MUSIC

Ting and Neil Morris

Illustrated by Ruth Levy

SEA-TO-SEA
Mankato Collingwood London

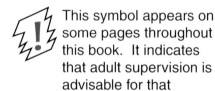 This symbol appears on some pages throughout this book. It indicates that adult supervision is advisable for that activity.

This edition first published in 2007 by
Sea-to-Sea Publications
1980 Lookout Drive
North Mankato
Minnesota 56003

Printed in China

Library of Congress Cataloging-in-Publication Data

Morris, Ting.
   Music / by Ting and Neil Morris (authors) ; Ruth Levy (illustrator).
     p. cm. -- (Sticky fingers)
   Summary: Provides step-by-step instructions for constructing different musical
instruments using craft techniques and readily available materials.
   Includes index.
   ISBN-13: 978-1-59771-027-5
   1. Musical instruments--Construction--Juvenile literature. [1. Handicraft.] I. Morris,
Neil, 1946-II. Levy, Ruth, ill. III. Title.

ML460.M83 2006
784.192'3--dc22

                                                                    2005057114

9 8 7 6 5 4 3 2

Published by arrangement with the Watts Publishing Group Ltd, London

Editor: Hazel Poole
Designer: Sally Boothroyd
Photography: John Butcher
Artwork: Ruth Levy
Picture research: Juliet Duff

Contents

Introduction

In this book you can learn about music and musical instruments both by reading about them and by having fun with craft activities. The information in the fact boxes will tell you about instruments from all over the world–their history, how they are used and what they are made of. You will learn something about modern music, too, including rock music's favorite instrument–the guitar.

Do you know how an orchestra is made up? At the end of the book is a plan to show the different sections of an orchestra, the instruments each section contains, and where all the different players sit. There is also a list of places to visit and books to read if you want to find out more.

So get ready to get your fingers sticky–making musical instruments as you read about them. Then you can make your own music!

Equipment and material

The projects in this book provide an introduction to the use of different arts and crafts media, and need little adult help. Most of the objects are made with throwaway household "junk" such as boxes, plastic bottles and containers, newspaper, and fabric remnants. Paints, brushes, glues and modeling materials will have to be bought, but if stored correctly will last for a long time and for many more craft activities.

In this book the following materials are used:

bamboo sticks
beads
braid (gold)
brushes (for glue and paint)
cardboard tubes
cellophane
cloth tape (colored)
cookie tin
corks
craft knife
curtain rings
cutting board
dowel rods
dry peas, beans or lentils
fabric (scraps)
felt (scraps)
felt-tip pens
foil (colored)
foil dishes
garden sticks
glass bottles
glue (water-based PVA, which can be used for thickening paint and as a varnish; strong glue such as UHU for sticking plastic, metal, and fabric; glue stick)

hammer
jar (for mixing paint and paste)
labels (self-sticking)
lids
liquid soap bottle, clean
metal nuts and washers
modeling clay
nails
paint (powder, acrylic, ready-mixed or poster paints)
paper (oak tag; cardboard; wax paper; tissue paper; newspaper; white paper;
pasta (in different shapes)
pencils
pencil sharpener
ping-pong balls
pitcher
plastic bottle
plastic tubing
plywood
popsicle sticks
ribbon
rope

rubber bands
ruler
sandpaper
scissors
shirt (old)
shoe box
stapler
straws
string
tacks
tape (Scotch tape; parcel tape; masking tape)
tape measure
toothpicks
varnish (PVA mixed with cold water)
wallpaper paste (fungicide-free)
water
wood
yarn
yogurt containers

Papier-mâché Tambourine

MESSY ACTIVITY

Here's a good way to get into the rhythm!

YOU WILL NEED:
✓oak tag ✓stapler ✓newspaper ✓fungicide-free wallpaper paste
✓PVA glue ✓yellow poster paint ✓ready-mixed paint
✓curtain rings ✓metal washers ✓beads ✓string ✓rubber band
✓tissue paper ✓cellophane or wax paper ✓scissors ✓water
✓brushes (for glue and paint)

1 Tear the newspaper into 1-in (2-cm) squares. Then mix the wallpaper paste as instructed on the package.

2 To make the frame of the tambourine, bend a strip of cardboard 25$\frac{1}{2}$ in x 2$\frac{1}{2}$ in (65 cm x 6 cm) into a circle, overlap the ends and staple them together.

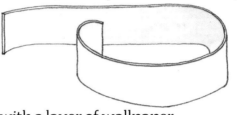

3 Cover both sides of the frame with a layer of wallpaper paste. Then press newspaper squares into the paste, smoothing out air bubbles and pushing the pieces together with your fingers. Then apply another layer all over. Add two more layers to the **outside** of the frame, pasting down any newspaper that is sticking over the top edge. Make sure the frame is bent into its circular shape and allow it to dry for a few hours.

4 Now turn the frame over to do the bottom edge. Apply one more layer of paste and newspaper to the inside and three more layers to the outside. Make sure that the bottom edge is even and that all the newspaper is turned in and pasted down. Check again that the frame is nice and round, and then let it dry. This will take a few days.

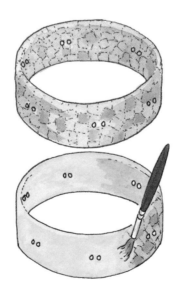

5 When the frame is completely dry, ask an adult to make six pairs of holes as shown, large enough for string to pass through.

6 Give the frame an undercoat of ready mixed paint before painting the whole thing yellow.

7 When the paint has dried, you can decorate the frame. Twist strips of tissue paper together and roll pieces into little balls. Dilute PVA glue with some water to a creamy consistency and soak the decorations in it before sticking them in position. Then varnish the frame with diluted PVA.

8 Cut six short pieces of string and thread a number of metal washers, curtain rings and beads on each. Push the ends of the string through the pairs of holes, and knot the string inside the frame.

The tambourine

The tambourine is a simple percussion instrument–that is, it makes a sound when it is struck or shaken. The main sound is made by hitting skin or plastic stretched over a wooden or metal hoop. There are also metal disks set in the frame, which jingle when the tambourine is shaken. Sometimes players rub their thumb around the edge to make a jingling sound. The tambourine is a very old instrument. Ancient carvings show tambourines that look similar to the ones we know. Today this instrument is widely used by the dancers of Spain and Latin America, and sometimes by pop groups.

9 If you want to add a skin to your tambourine, stretch a piece of cellophane or wax paper over the frame. Secure it tightly with a rubber band, and carefully cut off the overlapping edges. Now you can rattle and drum!

Shake, Rattle and Roll

1 Take two yogurt containers. Put a handful of dry beans into one container. Then join the two containers together with masking tape. Shake them to make sure you are happy with the sound.

YOU WILL NEED:
- 2 identical yogurt containers ✓ 2 identical foil dishes
- ✓ liquid soap bottle ✓ dowel ✓ dry peas, beans or lentils
- ✓ masking tape ✓ stapler ✓ colored foil ✓ ribbon ✓ white glue
- ✓ pasta in different shapes ✓ poster paint ✓ acrylic paint
- ✓ brushes (for glue and paint)

2 Glue on strips of colored foil to decorate your shaker.

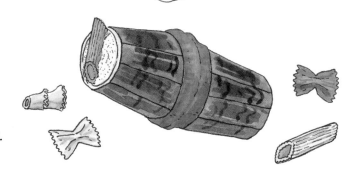

3 Paint small pasta shapes with thick poster paint. Cover the ends of the shaker with a layer of white glue and press the shapes into it. When the glue is dry, varnish the shapes with a second layer of glue.

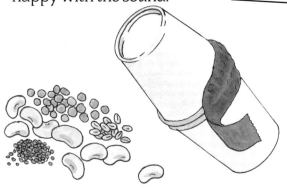

4 Make another shaker with foil dishes. First put in a mixture of peas and beans to vary the sound. Unfold the edges of the dishes and staple them together.

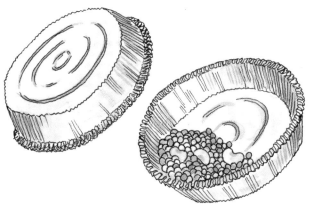

5 Decorate the sides with painted pasta shapes, peas, and lentils. Use plenty of glue to hold the decorations in position. Then glue a wide ribbon around the stapled edges.

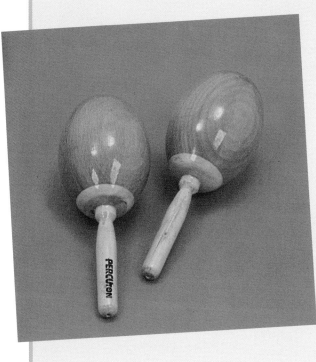

Maracas

Maracas belong to a family of musical instruments called idiophones. These are instruments made of materials that naturally make a sound when struck or shaken. Other idiophones are the xylophone, cymbals, castanets and triangle.

Maracas are instruments that you shake to make a rattling sound. They were originally made from the dried hollow shell of a gourd, which is a large fruit. This contained dried seeds or beans that could rattle about inside, and was attached to a handle. Maracas originated in Latin America, where they are used mainly in dance bands to give a strong rhythm. They are usually played in pairs.

Today maracas are often made of plastic and have lead shot inside, which gives a stronger sound.

6 You could add a rattle with a handle to your shaker collection. Pull the spout off an empty liquid soap bottle and put in some dried beans. Then push a stick into the neck of the bottle and tape it so that it fits tightly. Paint the bottle with acrylic paint. Now you can shake and rattle even louder!

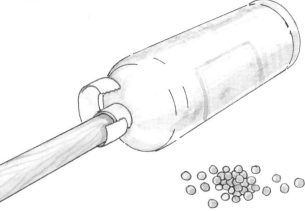

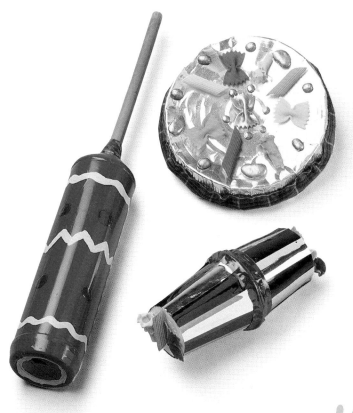

Shoe box Guitar

It is quick and easy to make your own simple guitar.

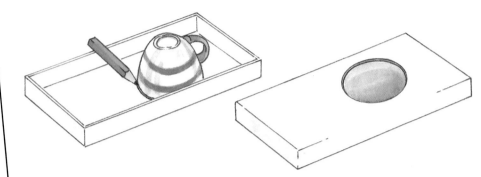

1 Cut a large round hole towards one end of the shoe-box lid. To make this easier, put a round object, approximately 3 in (8 cm) in diameter, on the inside of the lid and draw around it. Then cut out the circle.

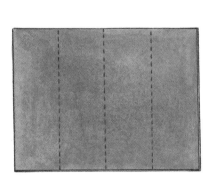

2 Tape the lid to the shoe box and cover the whole thing with oak tag. Don't cover up the hole you have just made! Then use felt tip pens to decorate the box. Make a circular design around the hole.

3 Next make two bridges for the guitar strings. Score two 3-in (8-cm) cardboard squares in three places as shown. Fold each square into a triangular stand and tape the edges together.

Attach a bridge to each end of the box with two strips of tape. Make sure that the bridges are in line with each other and the hole.

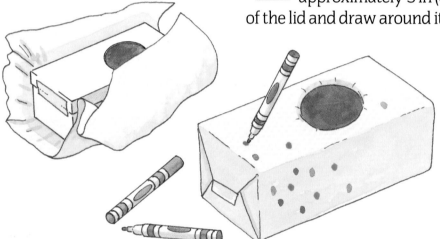

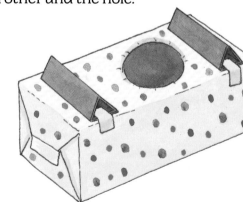

4 For best results, your four rubber bands should be slightly different sizes. Fit them carefully around the box and across the bridges. Check that each one is straight all around the box and not twisted. The biggest rubber band will be loosest and make the lowest sound, and the smallest and tightest will play the highest note. On a real guitar, the lowest string is at the top and the highest at the bottom.

Now you can hold up your guitar and pluck or strum the strings. You'll be surprised how good a shoe-box can sound!

The guitar
The guitar is a very popular stringed instrument. An early form of guitar was probably brought to Spain by the Moors many hundreds of years ago. Classical composers have written music for the guitar, and many works of the classical masters, such as Bach and Chopin, have been arranged for the guitar. In this century, the greatest classical guitarist was Andrés Segovia (1893-1987), who improved the technique of guitar-playing. The classical guitar is often called an acoustic or a Spanish guitar. It is used in the Spanish flamenco, a lively form of dance and music, and is very popular with folksingers. Chords can be played by strumming all the strings at once. Single notes can be played by plucking one string at a time, often using a plectrum. Rock groups prefer the electric guitar, which sends the sound through an amplifier and can produce more sounds than an acoustic guitar.

Pop Star

Follow these instructions to make your own pop star drummer.

1 Use a large plastic bottle for the head. A bottle with a flat front and back is ideal. Find a rod or tube that fits into the opening, or make a thin cardboard tube about 20 in (50 cm) long Push it into the bottle and tape the seam. Then find or make a wider, slightly shorter tube for the body.

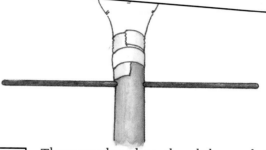

2 Then push a dowel rod through the thin tube to make the shoulders.

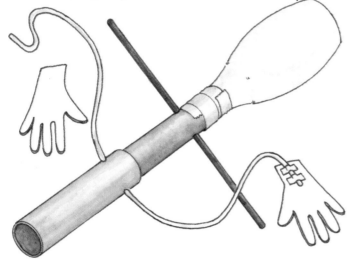

3 Thread a piece of thin rope through the body tube only, as shown. Carefully put the thinner tube inside the wider one—make sure that the rope doesn't get caught. To make hands, draw around your own hand and wrist twice on some cardboard and cut the shapes out. Tape the hands to the rope arms.

4 Use felt scraps or paper to make two big eyes, black eyebrows and a mouth. Stick them on the head. Add a nose, lots of yarn hair and a headband. You can also add some jewelry.

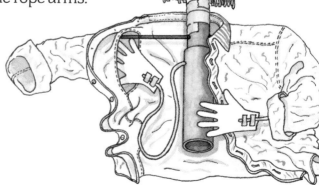

5 Dress him in a jazzy shirt. Pull the arms and hands through the sleeves. Button up the sleeves and collar.

6 To make a drumstick, twist tissue paper into a ball and stick it onto a straw. Make two and glue the straws inside the hands. If you want to be able to control the drumsticks, tie a thin stick to the back of each hand with string. You will need another person to control the head if you are going to work the hands.

Now all your pop star needs is a drum set! You can find out how to make your own drum on the next page. Now you've got the drummer, why not make a whole pop group?

Rock music

Rock is pop music with a heavy beat. It came from the American rock 'n' roll music of the 1950s. Rock with a very strong, loud beat is sometimes called heavy metal. The most important instrument in many rock bands is the electric guitar, and there are often three guitarists. The lead guitar plays the main tune, the rhythm guitar plays the backgrounds, and the bass guitar adds the lower notes. The band's drummer plays three types of drums, as well as the cymbals. The big bass drum is played with the foot, while the tenor drums and smaller side drums are struck with drumsticks. Many bands add keyboards — electric organ, piano or synthesizer. Pop singers are often idolized by young people. The first great rock 'n' roll star was Elvis Presley. His records sold millions in the 1950s and '60s.

Drum Away

1 You can use any round container for your drum. A deep cookie tin will make a big drum and a loud noise! If you want a smaller drum, a cocoa tin will do.

2 Take off the lid—we are going to replace it with a drum skin. The best thing to use for this is cellophane. Stand the cookie tin on the cellophane and cut a large square around it. Make sure that the cellophane overlaps the tin by 2 in (5 cm) all the way around.

3 Spread the cellophane over the open end of the tin, pull it tight all the way around, and make folds around the sides to get a tight fit. When the drum skin is taut, secure it with a rubber band. Then put parcel tape around the edges.

4 To decorate your drum, measure the circumference of the tin and cut a piece of red felt long enough and wide enough to go around it. Allow a bit of extra length so that you can make a neat seam. Glue the felt all around the tin.

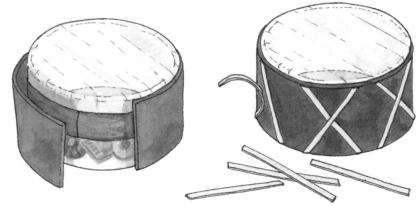

5 Cut strips of gold braid and stick them all around the drum as shown.

The kettledrum

Drums come in all sizes, and one of the biggest is the kettledrum, or timpano. This is different from all other drums in one important way. It is the only drum that can be tuned to make a definite note. Most symphony orchestras use at least three kettledrums. The skin of a kettledrum is stretched over a ring that is attached to a metal bowl. Some timpani are tuned by tightening or loosening screws around the top of the drum. Others are tuned by pressing a foot pedal and they are played using two sticks with soft heads.

6 Cut two narrow strips of blue felt to go around the top and bottom of the drum. Glue them in position so that they cover the ends of the braid.

7 You can make different drumsticks by winding tape, string or felt around one end of dowel rods or bamboo sticks. You can also stick a bead or cork to the end of a stick. Each stick will make a different sound on your drum. Don't play too hard or you might break the drum skin.

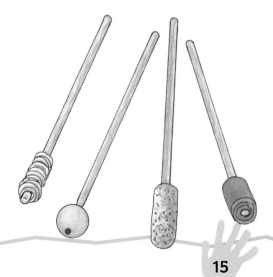

Kazoo Band

Make a set of kazoos in different sizes. Then you could get together with some friends and form a kazoo band.

1 Paint each tube a different color. When this undercoat is dry, add colorful patterns.

2 Cut a 5-in (12-cm) square of wax paper for each tube. When the paint is dry, cover one end of each tube with wax paper. Hold it in place with a rubber band.

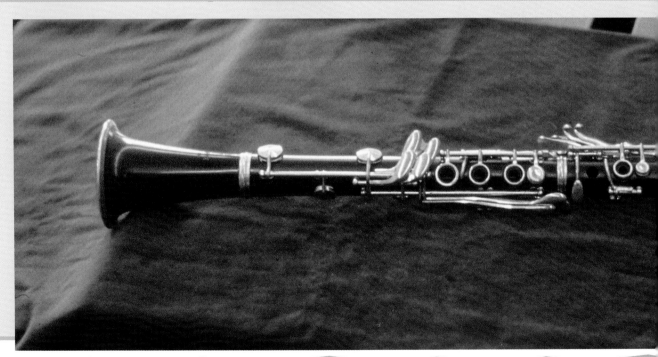

3 For your kazoo performance, hum or sing into the open end of the tube. A longer tube will make a deeper sound. If you have enough people for a band, the longer kazoos could make a background hum while the shorter kazoos play a tune.

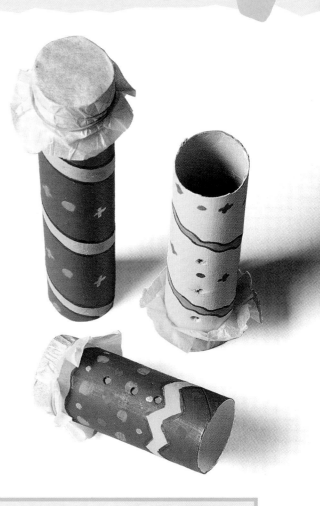

4 As a variation, you could make three holes in the tube of your kazoo with the point of a pencil. When you cover and uncover the finger holes as you hum, your kazoo will make a different sound.

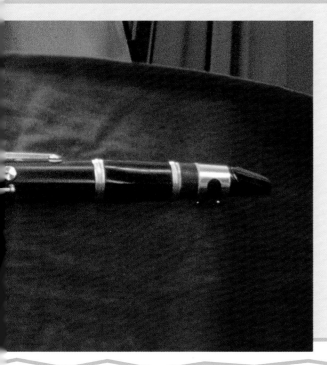

Kazoos and clarinets

The kazoo is a very simple musical instrument. A metal or plastic kazoo has a piece of thin paper covering a hole. This vibrates when the player hums or sings into the blow hole and a note is produced. Our own homemade kazoo works in the same way.

Woodwind instruments work in a similar way. The clarinet, for example, has a reed in its mouthpiece, which vibrates against a slot. The reed is usually made from natural cane, or sometimes plastic, or metal. The vibration produces the sound, which is changed by pressing keys that cover holes in the tube.

Ping-pong Conductor

Introducing the conductor of the ping-pong orchestra...

YOU WILL NEED:
- ✓ ping-pong balls ✓ yarn ✓ fabric scraps ✓ string
- ✓ dowel rod ✓ toothpick ✓ strong glue ✓ felt tip pens
- ✓ white oak tag ✓ 1 garden stick for each musician
- ✓ black and white felt ✓ masking tape ✓ scissors
- ✓ pencil sharpener

1 A ping-pong ball makes the conductor's head. Draw the eyes, nose, and mouth with a felt tip pen. Stick on some yarn hair and a felt moustache.

2 Sharpen a 12 in (30 cm) long dowel rod with a pencil sharpener and carefully push the pointed end into the bottom of the ping-pong head.

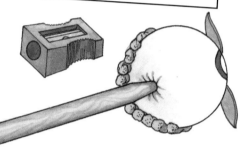

3 Cut a piece of string long enough for two arms. Tie and tape the middle of the string around the rod as shown. Draw four simple hand shapes onto white felt and cut them out.

4 The toothpick will be the conductor's baton, and you will use the garden stick to work the conductor. Place the toothpick and the rod between the two right-hand shapes, as shown, and stick them on. Then glue the hand shapes together and onto the string. Glue the left-hand shapes onto the other arm.

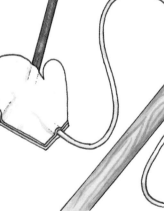

5 Roll two pieces of white oak tag around a pencil to make shirt sleeves. Fit the tubes over the arms and tape them with masking tape.

6 A square of black felt or fabric makes the conductor's jacket. Cut out a small neck hole in the center of the square, and stick the jacket to the dowel rod at the neck with masking tape.

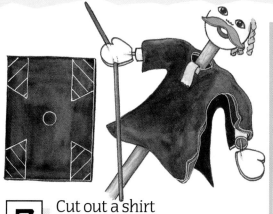

7 Cut out a shirt front from white oak tag. Add a black felt bow tie. Glue the shirt to the front of the jacket.

8 To work the conductor, hold his body in your left hand and the stick controlling the baton in your right hand. You could create a ping-pong orchestra to conduct by making musicians in the same way as the conductor. Why not make some musical instruments for them to play?

Conducting the orchestra

Imagine standing in front of 100 musicians and waving a small wooden stick to help them play a complicated piece of music in harmony. This is the job of the orchestral conductor, who must learn an amazing number of notes for every piece of music he conducts. His first task is to use his stick, called a baton, to beat time so that everyone plays at the right tempo. Music is divided into bars containing a number of beats, and the movement of the conductor's baton shows these beats. The conductor may use his other hand to signal to different sections of the orchestra. He may use both hands and even his whole body to show how loudly or softly a passage should be played.

Hosepipe Panpipes

1 Ask an adult to cut the tubing into eight pieces. The first piece should be 8 in (20 cm) long, the next 7$\frac{1}{2}$ in (19 cm), the next 7 in (8 cm), and so on. The eighth piece will be 4$\frac{1}{2}$ in (13 cm) long. *(If the tubing is curled up, soak it in warm water.)*

2 Decorate the pipes with pieces of colored cloth tape.

3 Assemble the pipes in order of size as shown. Wind a strip of cloth tape around one end of the pipes, and another strip around the other end.

4 Roll pieces of modeling clay into plugs that will fit inside the panpipes. Put a plug in the bottom of each pipe so that no air can get in. Blow across the top end of each pipe. If you want to make the sound of a pipe higher, push the plug higher up into the pipe with a rod.

Pipes

Panpipes date back over 2,000 years, and ancient examples have been found in most parts of the world. Throughout this time, they have been made out of many different materials—stone, clay, wood, cane, plastic, and metal. The instrument's name comes from an ancient Greek legend, in which the god Pan used a bundle of reeds to make music.

The idea for the oldest keyboard instrument, the organ, came from the panpipes. The first organ was the hydraulis, or water organ, invented in Alexandria in about 250 B.C. Air was pumped through the organ's pipes by forcing water into a drum. The Roman emperor Nero (A.D. 37-68) played this instrument.

Scottish bagpipes use a different method. A windbag is filled with air from the piper's mouth, and arm pressure on the bag forces the air through the pipes.

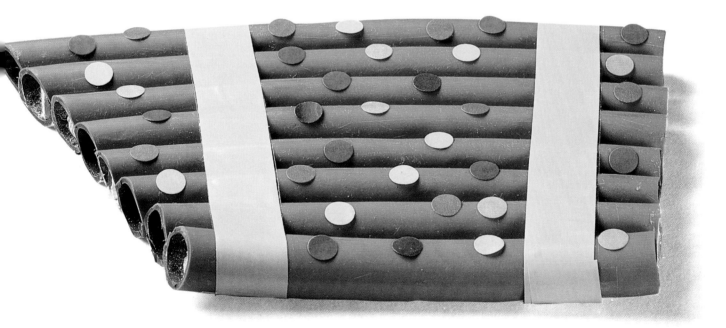

To play the panpipes, you blow across the top of them, rather than down into them.

Thumb Piano

1 Use a rectangular piece of plywood, 6 x 8 in (15 x 20 cm) and at least ¹/₂ in (15 mm) thick, for the board of the piano. Smooth the edges of the plywood with sandpaper.

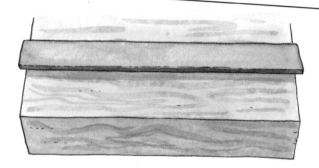

2 Ask an adult to cut a 1-in (2-cm) wide strip of wood, to fit across the width of the board. Again, smooth the edges with sandpaper.

3 Place 4 popsicle sticks at one end of the board so that they stick out over the edge at different lengths. Put the strip of wood over the sticks and press down to hold them in place. Now try twanging the sticks with your thumb. Move the sticks and the strip of wood until you are happy with the sound. Then tack them down in their positions on the board.

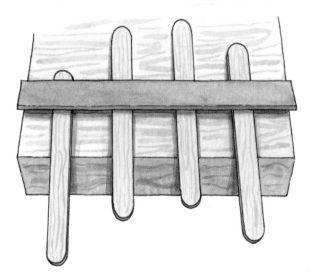

4 Now you need to nail down the strip of wood. Ask an adult to hammer the nails through the strip and into the board. First put a nail at each end of the strip. Check the position of the popsicle sticks again. Then hammer three nails in between the sticks.

5 Use poster paints to decorate the board with African designs. When the paint is dry, varnish the wood.

To play your thumb piano, hold it in both hands, or at the edge of a table, and twang the ends of the sticks with your thumbs. You'll soon be making your own African rhythm.

The African sansa

The sansa, or thumb piano, is a traditional African instrument. It is made of a number of metal or cane strips fixed to a decorated wooden board or box. There are from 8 to over 20 strips, or tongues, on each box. These are plucked with the fingers or thumbs while holding the sansa in the hands or on the lap. The tongues make a twanging or buzzing sound. Sometimes the sansa is put into the shell of a large gourd–a fruit–to make it louder. The sansa is played as a solo instrument, in groups, or with other instruments.

Pop-up Singer

1 For your pop-up card, fold the sheet of paper in half lengthwise, and then in half again. Make sharp creases.

2 Unfold the sheet. Draw a line 3 in (7 cm) from the bottom edge of the paper. The line should be 5 in (12 cm) long and in the middle of the sheet, i.e. 2 1/2 in (6 cm) either side of the centerfold. Place the sheet on a cutting board. Ask an adult to cut along the line with a craft knife.

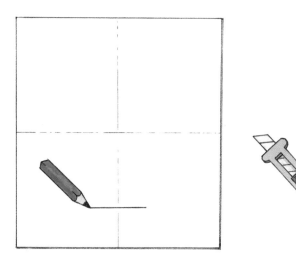

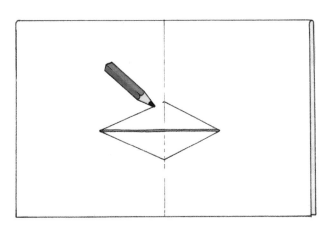

3 Make pencil marks on the centerfold, 1 in (3 cm) below and above the middle of the slit. Draw 4 lines in a diamond shape, as shown here. Ask an adult to score the lines by going over them with the tip of a pair of scissors.

4 Now you can make the pop-up mouth. Fold the paper in half again. Hold the half of the diamond above the slit and, while closing the card slightly, pull it out and fold it upward along the scored lines. Close the card with the top half of the mouth open. Then do the same with the bottom half of the diamond, and close the card with the whole mouth open.

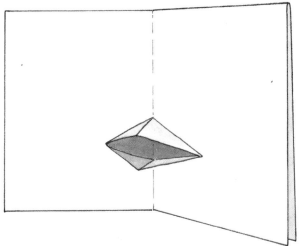

5 Open the card and draw a face around the mouth. Shade the inside of the mouth and paint the lips red. Add the eyes, nose and hair. You can copy this singer or draw your own favorite star.

6 Finally, you could draw a picture on the front of the card. Why not make some invitations for your very own karaoke party?

Singing voices

When we sing, we use our voice as a musical instrument. Women's voices are usually higher than men's, but they are not all the same. A high female voice is called soprano; a middle voice, mezzo-soprano; and a low voice, contralto (alto). A high male voice is called tenor; a middle, baritone; and a low, bass. Middle voices are the most common. Teachers build on a singer's natural gifts, and there are many methods of voice training. Some involve singing scales and exercises, while others concentrate more on singing actual songs.

Bottle Xylophone

1 Collect eight identical glass bottles. Arrange the bottles in a row and pour a different amount of water into each one.

2 If you tap the bottles with a pencil, you will hear that each one makes a different sound. Put the bottles in order, from the lowest note to the highest, and you have a simple bottle xylophone!

YOU WILL NEED:
✓ 8 glass bottles
✓ 8 self-sticking labels
✓ dowel rod
✓ wooden beads
✓ bamboo stick
✓ metal nuts
✓ pencil ✓ pitcher
✓ screw tops or corks
✓ water ✓ glue
✓ pencil sharpener

3 Do you know the scale "do, re, mi, fa, so, la, ti, do"? If not, you could ask an adult to help. Fill all the bottles nearly to the neck. Take the first bottle and call it "do". Pour a small amount of water out of the second bottle until it sounds like "re". Pour more out of the third bottle to make "mi" and so on.

4 When you have finished all eight bottles, you could label each one. Then close the bottles with screw tops or corks.

5 You can play your xylophone with one or two mallets. To make a mallet, sharpen the tip of a dowel rod with a pencil sharpener and glue a wooden bead on top. You can vary the sound by striking the bottles with different mallets. Try fixing a metal nut to a bamboo stick—but don't hit too hard with it!

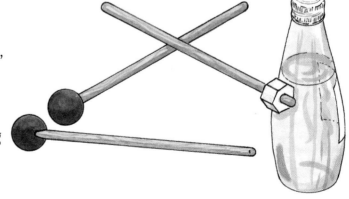

Xylophones

The xylophone is a set of wooden bars that are struck with mallets. The bars are arranged on a frame in the order of the notes they play. The longer or thicker the bar, the lower the sound it makes. Xylophones are common in Africa, where the huge log xylophone is played by two or three musicians. The simple leg xylophone is made of a number of logs resting on the player's outstretched legs, while another type has neck-straps so that it can be carried about as it is played. The marimba of Central America has resonators beneath the bars to make it sound louder and deeper.

Why not make up your own piece of music on the bottle xylophone? Get together with some friends and play some music on your homemade instruments. You could even record your compositions on tape!

The Orchestra

There are several different layouts for an orchestra. Here is one example.

Strings

The string section is the heart of a symphony orchestra, containing more than half the musicians. There are more violins than any other instrument, usually as many as 30 or more. They are divided into two groups: the first and second violins. The first violins play the highest pitched music, and the first violinist is the leader of the orchestra. In addition, there are about 10 violas, 10 cellos and eight double basses. Sometimes there are one or more harps, a piano, or a harpsichord.

Brass

Two to four trumpets and four to eight French horns play the higher brass parts. Two to four trombones and one tuba play the lower parts. Sometimes saxophones are added. The brass section can play more loudly than the rest of the orchestra put together.

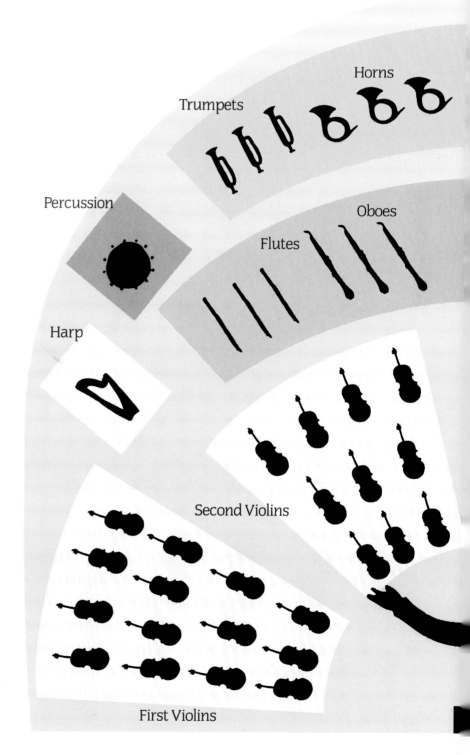

Horns

Trumpets

Percussion

Oboes

Flutes

Harp

Second Violins

First Violins

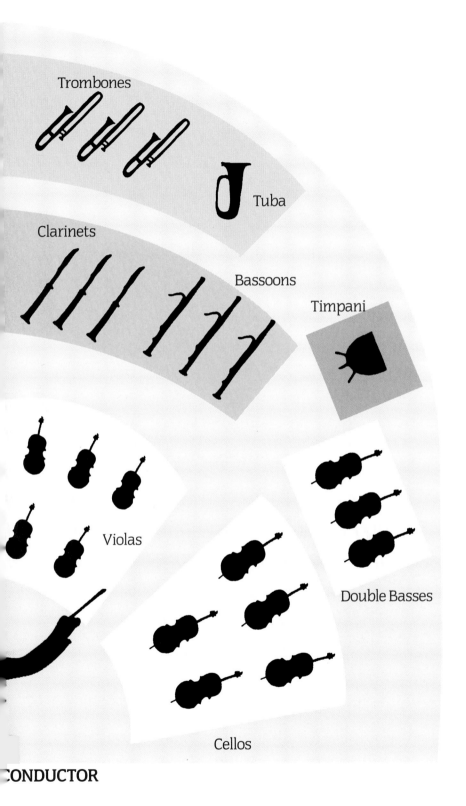

Trombones

Tuba

Clarinets

Bassoons

Timpani

Violas

Double Basses

Cellos

CONDUCTOR

Woodwind

In this section there are usually two to four flutes, oboes, clarinets, and bassoons. If needed, the woodwind musicians play other instruments too. A flautist (flute player) may change to the smaller piccolo, an oboist to the English horn, a clarinetist to the bass clarinet, and a bassoonist to the larger contrabassoon.

Percussion

This section includes any instrument that you can strike, rattle or shake. It normally includes two or more timpani (kettledrums), cymbals, a bass drum, snare drum, xylophone, and triangle. There might also be bells, a gong or a tambourine.

STRINGS

WOODWIND

BRASS

PERCUSSION

Glossary

acoustic guitar–often called a Spanish or classical guitar

bar–a group of beats in a piece of music

baritone–a middle male voice

bass–a low male voice

bass drum–a big drum with a low sound

baton–a conductor's small wooden stick

beat–the basic unit of rhythm in music, usually grouped in twos, threes or fours

castanets–curved pieces of wood that are held between the fingers and thumb and clicked together

contralto–a low female voice

cymbals–circular metal discs, usually brass, that make a loud noise when they are clashed together or struck with a stick

flamenco–a lively form of Spanish dance music

gourd–a large fruit with a shell

hydraulis–a water organ

idiophones–instruments made of materials that naturally make a sound when struck or shaken, such as maracas

karaoke–a form of entertainment in which people sing to a recorded background

kazoo–a simple instrument containing a thin piece of paper that vibrates with a buzzing sound when the player hums into it

kettledrum–a big drum that can be tuned to make a definite note

Latin America–areas of the Americas where Spanish or Portuguese are spoken — South and Central America, Mexico, and certain Caribbean islands

maracas–instruments that you shake to make a rattling sound

marimba–a Latin American xylophone with resonators that makes a deep, rich sound

membrane–a thin sheet, such as the skin of a drum or the paper that vibrates in a kazoo

mezzo-soprano–a middle female voice

Moors–a Muslim people of North Africa

panpipes–a number of reeds or whistles of different lengths bound together

percussion instrument–a musical instrument that makes a sound when it is struck, rattled, or shaken

plectrum–a small piece of plastic that guitarists sometimes use to pluck or strum the strings

reed–a thin piece of cane, metal, or plastic in the mouthpiece of wind instruments that vibrates to produce sound

resonator–anything that increases the richness of sound, such as the gourds or hollow pieces of wood or metal beneath the bars of a marimba

sansa–an African thumb piano

scale–a group of notes, in order, going up or down

Resources

side drum–a small drum with two skins and wires inside that produce a rattling sound; also called a snare drum

snare drum–a side drum

soprano–a high female voice

synthesizer–an electronic keyboard instrument, played like a piano, that can produce almost any type of sound

tempo–the speed at which a piece of music is played

tenor–a high male voice

tenor drum–a small drum with a high sound

timpani–kettledrums

triangle–a triangular metal bar that is struck with a metal stick to make a tinkling sound

Books to read

Music (Culture Encyclopedia Series)
by Antony Mason
(Broomall, PA: Mason Crest Publishers, 2002)

Music (DK Eyewitness Books)
(New York: DK Children, 2004)

Musical Instruments from A to Z
by Bobbie Kalman
(New York: Crabtree Publishing, 1997)

Story of the Orchestra : Listen While You Learn About the Instruments, the Music and the Composers Who Wrote the Music!
by Robert Levine
(New York: Black Dog & Leventhal, 2000)

Places to visit/Websites

Carnegie Hall
7th Avenue and 57th Street
New York, New York
Email: education@carnegiehall.org
Website: www.carengiehall.org

Cincinnati Art Museum
Eden Park
Cincinnati, Ohio
(513) 721-2787
Email: visitorservices@cincyart.org
Website: www.cincinnatiartmuseum.org

Delta Blues Museum
114 Delta Avenue
Clarksdale, Mississippi
(662) 627-6820
Email: info@deltabluesmuseum.org
Website: www.deltabluesmuseum.org

Library of Performing Arts
New York Public Library
at Lincoln Center
New York, New York
(212) 870-1630
Website: www.nypl.org

Louisiana State Museum
Jazz Collection
400 Esplanade Avenue
New Orleans, Louisiana
Email: lsm@crt.state.la.us
Website: http://lsm.crt.state.la.us/collections/jazz.htm

Metropolitan Museum of Art
Fifth Avenue and 82nd Street
New York, New York
Email: education@metmuseum.org
Website: www.metmuseum.org

National Museum of American History
Smithsonian Institution
12th and Constitution Avenue NW
Washington D.C.
(202) 633-1000
Email: info@si.edu
Website: http://americanhistory.si.edu/

Index

Additional photographs:
Alan Hutchison Library 23;
Clive Barda - P.A.L. 16-17;
Redferns 15, 19, title page;
Tony Stone Worldwide 7;
Zefa Picture Library 11, 13,
21, 25, 27